CW01306882

From a Child's Mind; To an Adult's Heart

Written by
Thop Brown

Edited by Anna Holston

authorHOUSE®

society. The elders called each other "sister" and "brother so and so," but we called them "Mister," "Mrs," or "Miss" so and so" with the first or last name as a sign of respect. I remembered famous singers visited different churches to put on a concert. One would think that as I became a teen my desire to go to church would lessen. It didn't. I thank God for Mrs. Smith who allowed me the chance to worship God even when I didn't understand my own desires. Though God called Mrs. Smith home when I was about fifteen, I still went to all of the services. I think Sunday school and the eleven o'clock services were the two most boring services of the day. I don't know whether I felt that way because of the mandatory services or perhaps because my sister, brothers and friends surrounded me, a deterrent from the service. I never could tell my mother what the Sunday school lesson was about, and I wasn't alone. I remembered mother was kind of upset with us because no one could tell her what the lesson was about. She made the mistake of asking us why we went to Sunday school if we weren't learning anything. In unison, all of us replied, "Because you make us go." Ironically, we had not planned to say those words that way. We knew better than to laugh at our mother. Oh boy! When we were alone, we couldn't stop laughing. As I looked back, Sunday school wasn't so boring after all. I remember how Mrs. Brown, the pastor's wife, gave up her time and worked so diligently to teach us the word of God. I didn't realize then that she "had a charge to keep," but I understand now. I am so glad that she didn't turn her back and give up on us as some people seem to have done with their children today. She had more than sixty children and two helpers at one time in Sunday school. If we became too loud, one of them would roll up the Sunday school booklet to hit that person on the head. That action made everyone get silent. We were very sensitive to the feelings of one another and didn't laugh at each other when someone was hit. We knew that the hit on the head could occur for any one of us the next time. As for the 11:00 A.M. service, I think that it was boring because during this service, people who called themselves Christians came to church. Some adults believed that service was the only time to come to see which one of us they could yell at or slap on the head for either talking, chewing gum or eating candy. The bottom line was that the adults helped the ushers keep the order in God's House and for this, I thank them.

Be Careful How You Treat God's Word

Some neighbors in this same community lived to the right of our house, on the right side of our street. We shared an alley. They had children the same ages as my two brothers, younger sister and me. They were a very nice family, but Mr. Donald forbade his family to go to church. Ms Brenda, his wife told my mother that Mr. Donald believed that Sunday was a day of rest, and his family should be home with him. She was a homemaker like my mother. All of the wives that had school age children in our neighborhood were homemakers except for Mrs. Mavis White. She had one child that stayed in the country with Mrs. White's mother.

Although Mr. Donald had every weekend off, Mrs. Brenda said "I tried to convince him to have family time on Saturdays, but he refused." Apparently, the other women looked to my mother for answers or maybe, they came to her simply because she was a good listener. Mrs. Brenda told my mother Mr Donald said; "I need Saturday mornings and afternoons to rest so I can go to the bar room on the Saturday nights to unwind from that week of stress at work."Mrs. Brenda said, "What he failed to understand was going to church on Sundays was her stress reliever." I felt sorry for Mrs. Brenda. Sometimes being an inquisitive child was hard because in cases such as these neighbors; my heart overflowed with sorrow for a person like Mrs. Brenda. She didn't deserved to be treated like that. I couldn't share my personal grief with anyone because I would have had to explain why I was listening to grown-ups conversations in the first place. I used to lock myself in the bathroom and shed tears for her and talk to God about her situation. God was truly a friend I could always depend on. I used a towel to muffle my cries, the price I had to pay for being inquisitive. Obviously, we lived in a loving but strange neighborhood. The adults went about their business as adults, but they showed their imperfections, which let me know they were only human. Take Mr. Donald Williams for instance. Every Sunday morning he had to let his family and the whole neighborhood know that he was the "god d---mn man of the house," and that what he "said goes." He would announce that no one in his house would be going to Church because Sunday was a day of rest. But every Sunday when my family left for Church, Mr.Donald's wife and their children would leave also. Although, no one seemed to pay attention to him, he would continue to yell, until we were out of sight. I asked my friend Linda if her father embarrassed her when he behaved in that manner. She reminded me everyone knows her father is still hung over from the night before and that she was used to his behavior. When I told her I would be embarrassed, if my father acted like that, she told me that when they returned from Church her father would usually be asleep on the sofa, chair or floor, wherever he was sitting when sleep hit him.

    Once Mrs. Brenda told mother that one Sunday the children and she had left the house to attend Church; Mr. Donald was still yelling, her name to ask her if she heard what he had said. She didn't think that he had realized they had left the house. Mom asked her how she could stand his yelling. Her reply was, "I ignored him and continue to do whatever I am doing. "She stated "It didn't hurt to let him think that he was in charge, as long as he kept his hands to himself."

    I can recall the final Sunday that everyone heard Mr. Donald objecting to his family's going to church. Perhaps, he had given his ultimate yell, the type of yell that he deemed so necessary that he had to take action with it. This particular Sunday, one could only speculate about the reason for his actions. He could have grown tired of his family's ignoring him and going to church in spite of what he'd said, or he had taken temporary leave of his senses. Whatever the reason, only God and Mr. Donald, knew it. When I think back on that day, I think about the book of Jeremiah chapter 1 verse 5. "God told

Jeremiah that he knew everything about him before he formed him." In other words, everything we do is predestined, so God had already ordained the action be taken at that precise moment. Mr. Williams had decided to take his actions a step further to get his point across. Not only did he tear up Mrs. Brenda's Bible page by page and step on it, but also he cursed God in the process. Mrs. Brenda was so upset by what happened that she didn't go to Church that Sunday. Instead, she came to our house in tears to tell my mother what had taken place that morning. She informed my mother how Mr. Donald thought that he had won because she and the children didn't go to Church. He had not realized that his wife was simply too upset to enter God's house. Later, he apologized to her and told her that she and the children shouldn't have provoked him to go so far. He claimed he didn't know what else to do to show them that he meant business, and that he knew no other way of to get their attention. This incident took me back to the scripture in the Bible about how Satan entered Judas Iscariot (Luke 22: 3rd verse) when Judas betrayed Jesus. As human beings we are not exempt from Satan's attack. No one should think that I am giving Satan any credit, because the book of Job in the Bible states; "Satan had to be given the power by God in order to touch Job" (Job 1:12). I honestly believe on that particular Sunday morning God gave Satan that same power to enter Mr. Donald that he had given him to enter Judas and to touch Job. How else would anyone explain the fact that a man dared to curse God and tear up His Holy Word, but that is my theory. I remembered hearing some of the elders saying God sometimes knocks people down to get their attention, in order pick them up so that they can do his will. This point brings to mind Saul on Damascus Road. When he was going to persecute the Christians, a bright light shined down from heaven and blinded him (Act 9:1-12). Mr. Donald thought that all was well and he was in control, because he had his family at home with him, as he demanded on that peaceful Sunday evening.

However, Mr. Donald was prepared to go to work on that Monday morning as usual. His mode of transportation to work was the bus the same mode of transportation for many of the men in the neighborhood. He had two ways he could have taken to get to the bus stop. He could have gone through his front door, which would have been closer to the bus stop or through the back fence that would have added an extra block. But as faith would have it, he chose to go out of the back door. According to some of the witnesses, he was on his way to catch his bus when Mr. Karl, one of the neighbors that lived on Vern Street called him. Years later, when I became an adult, I inquired about the incident that I vividly remembered. I was told that Mr. Karl and Mr. Donald talked a little but Mr. Donald told Mr. Karl that upon his return from work, Mr. Donald would meet with him that evening. No one knew what their conversations were about. My brothers, sister and I had just left for school. When Mr. Donald finished talking to Mr. Karl, Mr. Donald stayed on that side of the street, instead of returning to our side of the street. Mr. Karl had just stepped into the house to get ready for work when he heard a loud crash and people yelling for someone to call for an ambulance. When Mr.Karl ran to see what had happened, he saw that a tree that had stood in front of the barroom, some how had split in half and had fallen on Mr. Donald. Ironically during this accident there was no hurricane, lightning or hard wind blowing to cause the tree to fall, which had stood there for many, many, years. According to my mother, Mr. Karl had to be treated for shock. He blamed himself and believed had he not called Mr. Donald to his home, the accident would not have occurred. The barroom was the same one that Mr. Donald went into each Saturday to unwind. Of course, everyone was hysterical! This occurance was terrible to have happened to anyone. I can only imagine the feeling of helplessness and hopelessness that the adults felt while watching Mr. Donald lying in a pool of blood and in a state of unconsciousness. His wife had been inside with the washing machine on and wasn't aware of the ruckus that was going on outside. When one of the neighbors informed Mrs. Brenda, she went immediately to see about her husband. When she saw him bleeding severely, her knees weakened. As she cried hysterically, asking God to have mercy on her husband, apparently God honored Mrs. Brenda's prayer. Though, the act required only a matter of minutes before the ambulance, fire truck and police cars were at the scene, the time seemed like a lifetime, especially to Mr. Donald's wife. According to some of the witnesses, the men from the medical emergency unit couldn't understand how Mr. Donald had survived that kind of pressure. The branches from the tree were so big and heavy that firemen had to cut them before they were able to lift the tree from Mr. Williams. The fact that his neck wasn't broken, given the way the tree had fallen on him puzzled them also. Amazingly, often when one doesn't understand the word of God, one miss seeing the greatness of God. Apparently, no one among the medical personnel could see or understand that what had happened showed the power of God at work. Mr. Donald received a gash on right side of his head requiring 36 stitches, a broken collar bones, a few broken ribs, a badly bruised face, and a concussion. He remained in a coma for about four weeks as the doctors worked on him; many prayers were offered on his behalf. His doctor told his wife a miracle kept Mr. Williams from being paralyzed. Mr. Karl stood by the family's side throughout the whole ordeal. He continued to apologize to Mrs. Brenda and the children, despite of their assuring him that the accident wasn't his fault. He visited the hospital everyday after work until Mr. Donald came out of the coma. When Mr. Donald awaked, he understood the incident because he had heard the doctors and nurses talking. He told his wife how he had heard everyone's conversations, but he had been unable to respond. Also, he was aware of the pastor and some of the members praying for him even though he never set foot inside of a church. Mr. Donald asked his wife to tell her pastor that he needed to talk to him at his convenience. When Mrs. Williams' pastor arrived shortly after he received the massage. The pastor asked the visitors to leave the room, so he that could talk to Mr. Donald alone. After Mr. Donald thanked the pastor for praying for him, he told the pastor that he wanted to receive Christ in his life and that he believed God had used the incident to punish him for cursing Him and tearing up His holy word. Pastor Brown was unaware of all of these ideas until Mr. Donald told him. The pastor responded that Mr. Donald had to first admit being a sinner and to having had sinned against God before God would forgive him. Mr. Williams received Christ in his life that day. He admitted that he didn't know why God had spared his life because he didn't deserve it. He also admitted that he had never prayed because he never felt the need to pray. But now he could not seem to stop praying and reading his bible everyday. His wife started to join him in these sessions. As days passed he became stronger. Later he was released two and a half months after being hospitalized. Then he started going to church regularly with his family and eventually was baptized. Mr. Williams became a true believer of God. He attended church even when the rest of the family did not go. Over the years, he became a deacon in the church. The Bible states that "every knee shall bow and every tongue shall confess that Jesus Christ is Lord." I am so glad that God allowed me to see this conversion of Mr. Williams. This testimony for Him had a great impact on my life. Seemingly, every adult in that neighborhood had touched my life tremendously so that those impressions have stayed embedded deeply in my sub-conscience. I was between 12 or 13 years of age when this incident occurred. One would think after this ordeal I would have stopped being inquisitive, but I didn't. Eventually, the Williams family moved out of the community, but my family still saw them from time to time because Mrs. Williams' father lived in the neighborhood.

Skin Don't You Know Me

After the Williams family left the neighborhood, an elderly woman moved into their old house. She lived alone, her husband had passed some years earlier and she was childless. Mom befriended her, as did the other women in the community. My mother always volunteered us for such things as cutting other people's grass, going to the store and dusting for them. Mrs. Jackson was so kind. She wanted to pay us for going to the store or cleaning for her. My mom told her that our helping her wasn't an inconvenience, we were happy to do the chores for free. Oh well, we dusted her furniture, washed dishes, swept and mopped her floors, free of charge. One of my older brothers had returned from the military and lived with us for awhile. My mother introduced him to Mrs. Jackson. I don't think he liked Mrs. Jackson because he said that she looked like an old witch. When he returned, he picked up right where he left off; being our sitter. He convinced us that his suspicion about Mrs. Jackson's being a witch was right. He said that one night when he couldn't sleep, he had heard noises coming from outside. After he pulled the curtains back to see what the noise was, he saw Mrs. Jackson stepping outside of her skin. She started singing and dancing with her skin. According to my brother, she was singing "Skin don't you know me; ain't I'm your Master" over and over again. Although we had concluded that something was wrong with this guy, we still allowed him to make a fool of us. Were we a naive bunch? Yes. I remembered that before he left for the military, he had to watch us while mother went shopping. At that time the Williams' family were our neighbors. He would tell us to pick a fight with the children and say that we had better win. When Mrs. Brenda stopped the fights and took us to him, he told Mrs. Williams that he would take care of the matter and scold us in front of Mrs. Williams, while we stood there looking as dumb as ever. Of course, she was impressed with how he handled the matter. We knew not to say that he had told us to fight while Mrs. Williams stood there. When we returned to our home, he would apologize to us for scolding us and tell us that we had done a good job. As such naïve kids we believed everything our brother told us. For instance, although we knew eleven children were in our family, my brother told us that actually twelve children were in the family. He claimed he was a twin, but that his twin died. We used to call my brother, Poochie, which actually, I thought was his real name, I did not discover his actual name until I was twenty- one. Needlesstosay, he told us that his twin's name was Ochie. Of course, we believed him because every time our mother left, Ochie came to help Poochie to baby-sit us. Several things I noticed about Ochie were that he always set in the same place, wore the same clothes, only came around when my parents weren't home, and never talked. When I called these observations to the attention of my other siblings, they agreed. As a result, we asked Poochie about these things; his justifiable answer was that Ochie did not come around when our parents were home because he did not want to upset them and he did not have to change clothes because dead people do not change clothes. As logical as his answers seemed, they kept nagging me especially the part about Ochie's clothes. I had asked my brothers and sister to think about what Poochie had said. If Ochie, died as a little baby, why would he wear an adult man's clothes, unless people still grow when they die. I also wondered why Ochie had clothes and a hat like our father, but we could never see his face. As much as I wondered about all of these ideas we never could walk pass Ochie. Poochie always stopped us from going in the kitchen when Ochie was present. Poochie would stand in front of Ochie when we had to pass Ochie to go to the bathroom. His excuse was that his twin would be upset if we looked at him. In a big Cedar Chest where my parents kept their clothes.

Ochie would sit between that Cedar Chest and the wall on top of a bundle of clothes. He wore a pleaded shirt, dark trousers, dress shoes and a hat. He always sat with his legs crossed. While he was muscularly built, Poochie was skinny, a fact which should have given us some kind of clue right then and there. Nevertheless, we eventually asked my mother why she had not told us about our other brother. Our question shocked her. When she told us that we didn't have any other brothers, she became angry with my brother to learn that he had told us this lie. Of course he laughed about the situation saying he was just having a little fun with us.

There's a Thin Line between Chastening and Abuse

I could go on recalling the imperfections among the adults in our neighborhood, but I remember that not one person criticized the other. They weren't always in agreement with the method that some of the neighbors had chosen in chastising their children. One particular family in the neighborhood was abusive to their children. Although, the term "child- abuse" wasn't recognized in those days, it existed. I am quite sure the adults would have agreed that these parents were extremely hateful to their children. Someone should have reported these people to the authorities. There were no child protective services in those days. The parents seemed to have the right to chastise their children, and no one would infringe upon those rights, even if the child was beaten until he or she bled. This idea disturbed me to no end to see my friend, her sisters, and brothers in pain. The way their father beat them reminded me of how our forefathers were beaten by their masters during slavery. The Bazil children knew that they could depend on my mother to assist them, but ironically neither she, nor any of the other neighbors stopped or reported these parents to the proper authorities. The adults seemed to bandage up the open cuts on the children's back. Maybe doing so relieved their consciences. I could never understand how they even kept these activities undercover. Mr. Bazil forced his children to get naked and tied them up to the pole of their clothes line in the back yard. Brenda's older brothers and sisters were teenagers when their parents whipped them. I remember an incident when one of the older daughters had gotten away from her parents and ran to our house. My mother had taken her in, washed the blood off her back with peroxide and put bandages on her. My mother gave the girl some clothes to wear and comforted her until she'd cried herself to sleep. The adults would take care of the wounds, but I never recall any of them taking or even attempting to take the children to the hospital. During this period in the sixties segregation and the K.K.K. were on the up rise. There were no black police officers; therefore, black communities had to protect their own members. We lived in a close knitted neighborhood where the adults apparently believed in protocol. An unspoken rule among these adults was that if the children run off the adults would then be allowed to intercede and take care of them. One would think a conspiracy existed against the Bazil children, but none did. The adults thought they were doing the right thing by not saying anything to the outside world, not out of ignorance, but out of concern that the children would be separated from their parents. In those days, keeping the families together was very important. If child abuse had been, as noticeable then as it is today, Mr. and Mrs. Bazil would have been put under a jail with the keys thrown away. In fact, all the adults would have been put in jail the way children were chastised back then. Still I wouldn't trade being raised back then for all of the moneys in this world.

The Worst Kind of Abuse; Betrayal by a Parent

Incest was also a problem at one of the houses in our neighborhood. Unfortunately, Always among us is a child molester, even in an overprotective neighborhood like ours. They are wolves in sheep's clothing, sometimes handsomely dressed, hard working and often respected by the adults and children alike. Though this person was the stepfather, he still represented a father figure in the household. Mr. and Mrs. Johnson married when Mrs. Johnson's oldest son was ten, eldest daughter was nine and the baby girl was two. Mrs. Johnson had always been a happy lady. She and her husband appeared to be in love. She always said how blessed she was to find a man to marry her and raise her three children as his own. She worked at night, and he worked during the day. Therefore, he took care of the children while his wife worked nights. Both had weekends off. This family always enjoyed family outings on the weekends. Mrs. Johnson was so grateful to her husband for being such a good daddy that she obviously missed the unhappy look in her daughters' faces or perhaps the girls covered up their unhappiness because they wanted their mother to be happy. However, when the oldest daughter left home at the age of sixteen, her mother couldn't understand why she had left a good home. Mrs. Johnson asked my mother whether Mrs. Johnson's daughter had given a reason for leaving. My mother told her that she had not heard anything about her plans to leave nor did she seemed to be angry about anything. Mrs. Johnson realized that the children's father was strict with them and wouldn't let them go any further than our house, but she believed that he was only being protective of them. She speculated that her daughter might have been angry because he told their daughter that she was too young to date.

    As time went on the baby girl was developing rapidly. Then at the age of eleven, the youngest daughter became pregnant. She was nearly four months along before her mother took her to a doctor to find out why she was gaining so much weight. Mrs. Johnson was devastated when she found out that her baby was having a baby. Of course, her husband tried to blame the pregnancy on one of the neighborhood boys. Mr. Johnson obviously didn't know that the boys in our neighborhood were as naive as the girls were. Mr. Johnson knew that his daughter would have to tell her mother who had gotten her pregnant. He left home while they were at the doctor's office. upon their return, Mrs. Johnson noticed that the closet was opened and all of his clothes were gone. That discovery wasn't important. She had to get the truth out of her baby about who had done such a horrible thing to her. Her daugther didn't fully understand her mom's question; until her mother asked who had been touching her. She told her mother that her step-father had been touching her since she was nine. He had told her that this secret way showed that daughters and their fathers' had great love between them. He had also told her that every daughter showed her father how much she loved him in this way. However, he also urged her not to tell her mother or anyone else's mother because mothers didn't understand the type of love that girls had for their fathers. Mrs. Johnson ran through the neighborhood yelling "No-o-o-! No-o-o!" Some women in the neighborhood grabbed Mrs. Johnson to console her. They thought that she must of experienced death in her family. When she calmed down enough to tell them that her baby was four months pregnant by her husband. She asked, "How could he have done that to them. Daddies don't do things like that to their children. Then she called the police to report this crime because he had raped her daughter. When Mrs. Johnson's oldest daughter heard what had happened to her little sister, she came forth to tell her step-father had molested her since she was nine. She explained that she had left home for this reason. She had not told her mother because she saw how happy her mother was and believed her mother had deserved to be happy. Of course the older sister blamed herself for what happened to her little sister. She had not believed he was that sick to have touched a child that he had raised as his own since she had been two years old. About two weeks passed before he turned himself in to the police. He was given only five years for the rape of a minor. After the baby was born, Mrs. Johnson raised the child as her own. Her daughter never bonded with her baby son. Mrs. Johnson's daughter never had any other children. The man that she called "Daddy," had deprived her of any desires to have a child by the man that she would love at the appropriate time. No one really knew what she was feeling because she appeared to return to her old self. She seemed totally, to have block the whole episode from her mind as if it never happened. She really didn't see that baby as her baby boy. As I recall that time, I couldn't understand why the doctor did not require the girl to receive psychological counseling. We never referred to the baby as her son. I could only imagine what would have happened if we had. Her whole nine months appeared an out of body experience for her. A mind never fails to amaze me. It has all kind of coping mechanisms that allow us to deal with things that appear to be humanly impossible. This coping mechanism is the inner strength that God has instilled inside. I suppose that some people find their inner strength sooner then others. Though inner strength exists in everyone, some may never find it. That young lady continued to go to school and eventually graduated. The last time I saw or even heard of the father, his picture was on the front page of a local newspaper, and he was threatening to jump from a hundred and thirty floor building where a policeman tried to talk him out of killing himself. For those wondering whether or not he killed himself, I can tell you the answer is no. He did get a brief shot at fame.

Discipline plus Safe Haven

The neighborhood children enjoyed coming to my house because they felt secure and over all fairness from my mother. Although, she was the disciplinarian of the house, she made living in the house a pleasure. If an incident occurred in our home, she didn't get upset. She would call us together in a family meeting to tell us the reason for the gathering. The incidents in the house could range from the disappearance of two cookies while she was baking to someone putting the stopper in the drainage of the face bowl while the water was running. Though, she never accused anyone of us, she always judged fairly. She told us to look inside our heart to determine if we could live with ourselves, if we had been the cause of our sisters and brothers getting a spanking, when they had not been guilty. She would give us an hour among ourselves to talk. However, before she would leave the meeting, she let us know that if the guilty person / persons had not come forward after an hour had passed, than all of us would get a spanking. She would go outside so that she wouldn't hear our discussion. Most of the time her method would work; the guilty person would break down and confess long before our hour was up. Later, my mother told the rest of us to go outside; the guilty person to remain right where he or she was standing. Of course, we listened for that person to start crying from the spanking, but we would not hear anything. Mom would tell the culprit how brave he or she had been coming forth, sparing his or her sisters and brothers. Then she gave that person her speech about not taking anything without permission.

She would explain this form of stealing, even when occurred in our home. At times all of us have gotten a spanking because the guilty person didn't come forward. My older brother would never admit to my mother that he had done anything; However, during our meetings he would admit to us the he was the guilty one. My mother never knew because he did not admit his wrongs to her. As a results, all of us could get a spanking. He informed us that if we squealed on him, he would beat us up. No one would say anything, because we knew that my mother would have killed my brother for his dishonesty. At those times, all of us received a spanking. Finally, my brother became old enough to be drafted into the Army, Oh! Happy Day for the four of us. What are the odds of having a brother that makes up a twin brother to scare us half to death and another one that enjoys getting us into trouble with our mother, having the same birthday? Did you say impossible? These two clowns birthdays occur on the same day, five years apart. Can you believe that! Still I love them and wouldn't have trade them for the world.

Skeletons in the Closet

"Skeletons in the closet" is an old saying that the elders used when they were referring to "a family's or community's secrets." I realized that all of those old sayings had some sort of meaning to them that made a lot of sense, once they were explained. I was a teenager when I had the opportunity to ask my mother (during one of our conversations), what did the phrase "Skeletons in the closet" mean? She told me that it meant that; "There is a family secret that was supposed to stay within the family." This secret may be anything from a disabled child to a teenager getting pregnant out of wedlock. Sometimes, when a teenager became pregnant out of wedlock, she would be sent away to relatives until the baby was born. A logical excuse was given for the teen's sudden departure, and that excuse was accepted. Today, one might wonder why a person would have to give anyone an excuse for what's going on in his or her home. Unlike, today societies the neighbors were closely knit and the absence of one child is noticed. After the teenager had given birth, she and her baby might stay with the relatives for about a year. Then several months after the teenager arrived home, a small child would appear and another excuse explained that the teen's mother had to raise that child as the teen's sister or brother. In those days, a family's honor and the protection of the children meant so much to the adults. They would go to extreme measures to keep that honor and to protect their children. The parents of the unwed pregnant teenager believed they were protecting her from embarrassment, an act which I thought showed the true meaning of unconditional love. This form of "skeleton in the closet" extended outside of our community. Surely, the adults would vent their disappointments with the act committed by that particular teenager among themselves, but they kept the news from the other children. In actuality, the skeleton these adults thought they were keeping in the closets from the other children in order to spare that teenager from embarrassment was often exposed when the pregnant teen told her friends. I don't think the adults realized that the same respect and compassion that they had one for the other, they had taught us to have among ourselves. If someone became pregnant that person would tell the other teens that she had been stupid and had become pregnant. She would cry, but we knew how to console her. We often talked about the little white lies the adults would come up with, to protect us. We realized how blessed we were to have parents who protected us. A scripture in the bible, (Genesis 20:20) revealed how Abraham lied when he said that his wife Sarah was his sister. The scripture made me realize that sometimes a little white lie seemed necessary to protect the innocent. We knew before hand, which family would have had an imaginary death and who had to raise a baby as their own child. We would never disrespect parents or call them liars. In fact, they did raise the child as their own until the young parents graduated and got married. Even if the child's parents chose not to marry or chose to go to college or join the military, the grandparents would be supportive of them. Usually the girls' parents took on the responsibilities of raising the child until the mother was able to take care of her child financially.

One particular teenager in our community became pregnant. This girl wasn't allowed to play with us, because her mother thought that there were too many boys in the neighborhood. This family had moved to our neighborhood about three years before the teen became pregnant. Unfortunately, her mother had not realized that we were innocent teens that liked wholesome recreation like softball. We were teenagers, who didn't realize that our private parts could be used for anything other than to eliminating wastes. After her daughter gave birth to triplets, the mother realized that if she had allowed her children to play with us, they might have been as naïve as we were. We didn't know what we could have been learned. This experience might have been a blessing in disguise because Cherlyn could have introduced us to sex. We were a group of teens that were over protected by our parents, but, we still given some liberties. Cherlyn's mother, on the other, hand allowed her to do almost nothing so she took secret liberties that were life changing.

In those days, only a few blacks believed in abortions, but sometimes if necessary a midwife performed abortions. The same midwife also delivered babies. I was amazed that those women had no medical background, but they delivered healthy babies most of the time. Such actions are surely examples of the women of old having a godly wisdom. Despite being uneducated, midwives were miraculously these women knew how to deliver a baby and correctly tie an umbilical cord. This godly wisdom surpassed the education taught by humans and that guided the midwives. In some cases, the midwives were the next thing to medical doctors because most blacks could not afford to go to the doctor. The ones that could afford to go to the doctor were sometime refused care because of the color of their skin.

When the baby was ready to be delivered, the midwife would go to the teenager wherever she lived. Midwives were trustworthy and respected for their wisdom and knowledge.

Then there were some members of families that had the "if it feels good to you do it" attitudes. They showed no regard to the embarrassment their actions may have caused other members of their families in the process. These too were considered skeletons in the closet. The person who caused the embarrassment to the family was in her own little world and did not realize that other members of their family were actually aware of her little secrets. Even though, this idea is supposed to be a family secret, there was always one family member who broke the code of silence. That person believed she or he needed to tell the secret, and in the process exposed that family's secret. I honestly don't think that these exposures were done maliciously. Sometime the incident was so devastating that the family member needed to talk about it. Ironically, the "skeletons in the closet," in those days, had been let out of the closet, so everyone except the family member who thought the little secret is well covered. People sometimes look at another person and treat them differently when they learn of "the skeletons in the closet." There were so many skeletons in the closet in our community. The adults in the neighborhood were a family within a family. I could only speculate that the reason they shared their deep dark family secrets among themselves was to relieve some of the burdens the secret caused. Surely there were many more skeletons running around our neighborhood than my little inquisitive ears had heard.

One of the secrets that came across my ears was about my aunt leaving a baby boy in the hospital after giving birth because the baby was not fathered by her husband. Can you imagine coming across such information at the age of ten and not being able to speak about it? My inquisitiveness has caused me to shed many silent tears because of the things I've seen or heard and wasn't able to tell anyone. I couldn't take a chance on telling the one sister and two brothers I had grown up with, even though we were closely knit. However the older of the two brothers was very smart and observant; I might add. He noticed that I had been crying and asked me what was troubling me. Telling him nothing was wrong didn't stop his persistance. Before I responded his question, we would perform our little ritual. If something very important confronted us that we couldn't talk about in detail, we would say this phrase together, "what we hear, see or say, when we leave let it stay," and we honored that saying. When I told him what I had heard, he became stunned and angry. We vowed to find our cousin when we became adults. One day my youngest sister heard us talking about the secret. We didn't like to let her in on secrets because she would keep secrets only until she became angry with us; then she would tell our mother everything. Since we were teenagers then. I thought that maybe my sister had matured because she managed to keep her word. No matter how angry my brother and I made her, she didn't mention anything to our mother.

One day I stumbled on our family secret. In the summer of 1964, someone knocked on the door. When my mother opened the door, I could see two white policemen and a white woman, whom I found out later was from Social Services. My mother asked how could she be of help. I could hear the fear in my mother's voice. We weren't accustomed to police officers knocking on our door. The lady responded by introducing herself and stating that she was from the welfare office. Of course my mother was even more puzzled because no one in our neighborhood received welfare. The woman obviously noticed the puzzled look on my mother's face and explained that her visit wasn't about anyone receiving benefits. She said she had reasons to believe that someone at our address had given birth to a baby. Before the woman could finish what she was saying, my mother proudly blurted out that the information was correct, that her daughter had recently given birth to a baby. I was peeking from behind the curtains and could see what appeared to be a satisfying look on the two officer's faces as well as the lady's as they looked at each other. I recalled thinking that something wasn't right with what they were saying. I thought the situation was over mother's head. Then the lady explained to my mother that there had been a baby boy left in the hospital. The mother had given a phony name and our address. Then my mother became very defensive explaining that her daughter had brought her baby with her, but that she had given birth to a baby girl. The social worker asked my mother if she knew who would do such a thing, and why someone would use our address. Even though my mother replied "no," my mother suspected that my Aunt Sarah was the person that they were looking for. Without their knowledge the social worker and the police officers had just cleared up what my mother and some of the other neighbors had suspected but that my aunt denied that she had been pregnant. Several of the neighbors had asked my Aunt Sarah if she was pregnant, but she had denied this claim. Her husband was a seaman, a job that often kept him away from his family. He was gone about six to eight months out of a year. Once we had enjoyed a family gathering upon his return home. He obviously noticed that my aunt was gaining weight, and made a statement about her getting a little fat around the belly in front of everybody. I have never forgotten how angry she had gotten with him. He told her that he was just joking around, but my aunt's daughters knew she was seeing another man while their father was away. His statement seemed to have fallen right in place with her plan. Because she already had planned not be intimate with her husband. While he had been in town for two months, my cousin reported that my aunt slept in a guest bedroom during his time at home. My aunt had told them never to tell anyone, but my cousins told me. Apparently, my aunt had planned everything. She knew that her husband would be away on the ship when she gave birth. All she had to do was keep denying the fact that she was pregnant to my mother and the other neighbors. It seemed that she kept all of her prenatal care appointments using an assumed name. Soon I realized that my aunt was one of the most devious, and not to mention, evil people that ever lived. When I became an adult I confronted one of my older sisters, Tammy with the fact that I knew that my aunt had left her baby boy in the hospital. Of course after she recovered from the shock of my knowing what was supposed to be a skeleton in our family closet, she told me her version of what happened. I realized that this incident had occurred many years ago, but the fact remained that I have a cousin out there some where. My question to everyone was, "Why wasn't my aunt reported?" I received the same response from everyone: They had to think about the fact that Aunt Sarah's children would have been without a mother if she had gone to jail. My mother recalled that my aunt had worn a big coat even on warm days inside the house. She remembered that my aunt walked bent forward so that the coat could hang loose. She remembered that my aunt endured ridicule about wearing the overcoat with no attempt to take it off in the house. After awhile, she stopped coming to my mother's house. Then one day she came to my mother's house with her hair dyed red and cut short the way my sister had always worn her hair. She offered my sister a present; it was the red boots that my aunt had always worn. Tammy bore a remarkable resemblance to Aunt Sarah and Aunt Sarah was aware of that fact. According to Tammy, my aunt knew Tammy would accept the boots because Aunt Sarah knew Tammy had always admired them. Although Tammy had noticed that my aunt no longer wore her coat and had a flat stomach, Tammy did think that Aunt Sarah could have had a baby and given it away. Aunt Sarah was about three years older then Tammy who had given birth to a baby girl. Tammy remembered that my mother had told her to get rid of the red boots that my aunt had given her. My mother remembered that the social worker had been looking for a black female, with red short hair. One of the nurses remembered seeing that the woman wore red boots when she came in to have the baby. Tammy stated how deceived she had felt. This perfect example shows how everyone around a person knows his or her secret, but that particular person thinks that her deep dark secret is truly a secret. No one ever confronted my aunt. When I asked my mother what ever became of the child, she didn't know. After my sister had proved that she had given birth to a baby girl and that the child was living with her, the inquiry ended. Though the neighbors knew from my mother about the visit from the policemen and social worker, no official report was made. Since our neighbors didn't like Aunt Sarah, they tolerated her because she was my mother's sister. Aunt Sarah must have felt a sense of guilt because when my uncle told her the he was to be promoted to a job not requiring him to be on the ship, he also said they would have to move to New York. He had some relatives living in New York, so uncle and aunt eventually moved there. My uncle seemed to resent not being on the ship. I don't know if he ever found out about the baby, but I found out years later that he knew that one of the girls was not his child. This secret is another one of Aunt Sarah's, but never realized that other people knew about. My aunt continued to be the loving wife she had claimed to be for years. The more I saw my aunt when she visited us, the more contempt I felt for her. However, as I grew older the contempt that I felt as a child turned into pity. My cousins and I kept in touch over the years. They informed me that my aunt's life wasn't as good as she pretended. They told me that their father would drink and frequently beat their mother. He had broken her arm and knocked out her teeth. Later, she lied and told my mother that she had been in an automobile accident, where her arm had been broken and where she had loss some of her teeth. My mother went to New York to be with her sister.

 As for the baby incident, I waited until I was well in adulthood to inform my mother or some of the other neighbors with whom I could talk. I received the same initial startled looks on each of the faces when I approached each one. The question that they always asked me was, "Where did you hear that?" I simply confessed how intrigued I was with the cohesiveness that was present among the adults. Also, I told them that I was curious about their reasons for congregating so much. In the process, I had to overhear some of their conversations that I knew I should not have heard. I had heard the police officers, the woman from social service and my mother talking when the incident occurred. I never breathed a word of what I heard to any of the other children, except that which I told my bother and sister. I kept the information imbedded in the back of my mind until I became an adult. I told whomever I was talking to at the time that I needed to understanding why some of the skeletons from the neighborhoods' closets were kept such a secret, even though the adults disapproved of the behavior. Most of the answers I received were the same; "I could not have lived with myself if I knew I was the cause of that mother or father being taken away from their children; "Or that "I didn't report it because it would have hurt his or her parents, brothers or sisters;" As I think about all that had transpired over my young life, and as I meditated on the actions that the adults took or did not take, I realize that I have no malice toward anyone. However, some things occurred as a result of a lack of knowledge.

In spite of it all the love and devotion the grown-ups had for each other back then, the very act of God would be required to produce that kind of love in neighborhoods today. Most of the neighbors today don't even know the names of the people living next to them. The society today is so individualized that it never knows when a crisis has arisen at the neighbor's front door or some simply don't care. I found out as I grew older that all of us have some kind of skeleton in our closets. There are skeletons that only chosen family members know about. Some of the reasons that only chosen family members knew about them, ranges from some family members being too weak to handle the news or not old enough to understand to some being too talkative to maintain the secret or secrets.

Among all of the skeletons in the closet, the one that I thought was the most sensitive and the cruelest involved families with physical handicap relatives. The handicapped relatives were moved into the house late at night when there weren't many people stirring about. I thought that act of sneaking members into the house was cruel. One of our neighbor's child was mentally and physically handicapped. How did I find out about the child if the family concealed him from the rest of the world? No, I wasn't snooping this time. In fact, quite some time had passed before I found out. The family had been living in our neighborhood almost two years before I found out about him. Can you imagine that? I became close friends with his sister who never mentioned that she had a handicap brother. One day after we were playing in her yard, she invited me inside to get some water while her parents weren't home. While inside I kept hearing a noise that was scaring the life out of me. I asked Jane about the noise. She told me to sit because she wanted to tell me something that I must promise not tell the other children. I promised, she told me about her brother, who was actually her twin. When I asked to see him, she took me to the room were he was sitting in a big rocking chair, his legs tucked under him. She played with him, he smiled and reached out for her, while drooling as a five or six months old baby would do. When she introduced me to him, I was afraid at first, Jane told me not to be afraid because he was just like any other baby. I gave him my hand and he smiled at me while making that noise that I had heard earlier. She said that he was happy like that all of the time. Although, he was actually thirteen like us, he had the mind of a five or six month old baby. We kept the secret about James, for a long time. But, one day when Jane and I thought we were alone I asked her about him and her mother heard me. She called us in the house to ask Jane how I knew about James. When Jane told her mother the truth, the mother realized that I had known the family secret for almost seven months without telling anyone. Therefore, I became an honorary member of the family and was allowed to come in and eat dinner with the family. Jane's mother told my mother that I knew about James. My mother was amazed that I had not mentioned this news to her. I told my mother that I had promised my friend that I wouldn't tell any one.

James was not the only handcapped boy in the neighborhood; we grew up with two other handcapped boys. They were able to get around; one of the boys (Joe) functioned as a normal child. Of course the adults never talked about these things. An unspoken rule existed that forbade children from asking questions or staring at another human being. There were rules, that I always managed to break, I might add. I didn't stare but I sure asked questions, especially if something seemed out of the ordinary. How does one learn unless they ask questions? I didn't realize that Joe was handicapped until I had gotten older. I just thought he was a disgusting big head, aggravating little boy who enjoyed working on the girls' nerves. He had that mastered, especially working my nerves. One day, he asked me if I was going to miss him when he went into the hospital. Of course this question raised my curiosity, I needed to know why he was going to the hospital. He told me that he was going to get the metal plate changed in his head. I think that was the first time I really gave Joe any of my time. As he talked about his operation, for the first time, I noticed the scar in his head. He told me that he had been born with water on the brain. The more he told me about himself, the more I understood why he acted the way he did. I felt a sense of compassion (not pity) coming over me for him. Later, his operation was successful, and his family eventually moved out of the neighborhood.

On the other hand, Mike who was a deaf mute was also aggravating. The problem with Mike was that we didn't know how to communicate with him. He didn't live in our neighborhood, but his cousin did and he often visited his cousin's family. His cousin, Larry played a big part in the way Larry acted. He knew that we couldn't communicate with Mike, so he perform sign language to tell Mike that the girls wanted him to kiss them or that we wanted him to be our boyfriend. We would run from him and he thought that we were playing with him. I had become frustrated that when Mike came around, I wouldn't go outside. Mom, being in tuned to us noticed that something was wrong. One day she asked me why I was not outside on such a pretty day. I told her that Larry would tell his cousin the girls liked him and wanted him to kiss them. She became so angry that she told Larry that if he didn't get his cousin to leave the girls alone they wouldn't be allowed to visit any more. He was obedient and told his cousin that the girls did not want to be kissed. They continued to visit but all Mike did was stare at us. As I reflect on the past, I could only imagine what must have gone through Mike's mind. I imagine that he wondered why the girls played with the other boys but never included him. Sometimes, I would observe Mike when he wasn't staring at me. He seemed to have such a sad look on his face. Then I would see him smiling when he saw one of us doing something funny. To know what we must have put him through and the fun we deprived him of having, saddens me simply because we didn't know how to communicate with him. I wished that someone had taught us sign language or just the basic alphabets so we could communicated with Mike. The fact that the adults didn't see the need for us to communicate with the deaf mute (deaf and dumb as the hearing impaired were called) was so sad. Didn't the adults (especially his mother) realize that Mike had feelings too? I often wondered why his mother allowed him to be exposed to other children without getting out there with her son and teaching us how to communicate with him. I had so many questions to ask as I reflect on my life with Mike and Joe. Since these questions will never be answer, I am forced to draw my own conclusions. I concluded that Joe's handicapped condition, because ignorance, not out of malice, deprived all of us. I am a living witness that what happens in children's lives follows them through adulthood if the issue is important to them. There are always going to be situations in one's life that will bring back childhood memories. I made a vow to at least learn the alphabets in sign language, and today, I know the sign language alphabets and a few words. I am glad I learned these because I have had the opportunity to work with a hearing impaired person. Even today, with laws that protect the rights of the disabled, many are still being isolated on the job because people lack the knowledge to communicate with them. I wondered who were the real dummies- the hearing impaired or society? Perhaps in those days, society shunned the whole family if a handicapped person was part of the family. Finally, when the Disability Act of 1964 was established, it opened a lot of doors for the disabled. I don't know what happened to Joe and Mike, but I hope that they were able to take advantage of the Disability Act of 1964 and received the education that they desired and deserved. My prayer is that their lives are successful. Now that the disabled are finally being recognized as human beings, Surely many families with disabled relatives are relieved. Now they can get an education and demand to be treated as human beings. Although, ignorance still prevails, society is being educated to adjust to the disabled person in our society. Prejudice towards the handicapped person has been noticed and finally was dealt with accordingly. There will always be some form of prejudice base on a general lack of knowledge when it relates to disabled people.

The Neighborhood Children in 50's and 60's

We were children that Paul addressed in the Bible (I Corinthians chapter 13 verse 11) he stated "When I was a child I thought as a child, I spoke as a child." I might add we played as children with not a worry in the world. As I recalled my life as a child I think the children in my neighborhood can go down in history as the most naïve children in our generation. We had so much faith in our parents and the other adults. We believed that an adult didn't lie, a typical normally sentiment in our neighborhood. The adults knew that we depended on them, and they did not betray our trust. However, we came to realize sometimes the adults had told us little white lies for our own good. Often we were too naive or had too much faith in them to question their authority. My mother had the most influence on the neighborhood children since our house was the meeting place. We had the only television and movie projector in the neighborhood. My mother always took the time to play ball with us while the other adults looked on and laughed at her attempts to keep up with us. She always kept our minds active by playing trivia games with us, especially during the summer time. This woman would always claim that she didn't get pass the first grade. We could never prove that she did get pass the first grade because the other adults backed her up 100%. Of course that, fact aroused my curiosity, because I couldn't understand a person with such limited education was so interested in developing the mind and knew so much. But, as always we simply didn't push the issue. Her educational background was the first little white lie. The fact that my mother had never left the house but seemed to know everything we did and everywhere we were was also a mystery to us. When we confronted her with the fact that she knew what we had done or where we had been without leaving the house, her reply would always be "a little bird had told her." The neighborhood children often told us how much they would like to meet my mother's little bird and kill him, we agreed with them wholeheartedly. This little bird seemed to be the nosiest bird that ever lived. I realized that we were the silliest children in our generation because we used to have serious discussions about silly things like my mother's little bird. Sometimes we allowed our imagination to run away about what we would do if we ever met the little bird. The discussion became so ridiculous that we had to laugh at ourselves. I am surprised that none of us became comedians because we kept each other laughing all of the time.

    The more I recall my upbringing, the more I realized that my mother was the culprit of the white lies. I think that a mutual agreement existed among the adults but she would be the ideal person to relay the lies to us. Surely, they colluded on this particular lie just as they conspired about everything else. We loved to get up early on Saturday morning to do our chores and go outside. The children congregated at my house every chance they got. We played such games as rock teacher on our steps, played red light, giant steps or Simon says in front of our door. Thinking that my mother wanted to sleep late on Saturday mornings never occurred to us or that she may have gotten tired of the other children coming to her house everyday. Perhaps, because she never gave us any indication that she was tired of the other children, she appeared to derive great joy from having children around her. In fact, Later as an adult, I inherited her spirit of having lots of children around me. It seems like the more children I have around me the more joy I have. Nevertheless, I think my mother enjoyed playing little jokes and watching us take the bait. We were so trusting of her that we fell for the joke every time. Case in point, there was an old white man who used to pass through our neighborhood on Saturday mornings. We weren't accustomed to seeing white people in our neighborhood unless they were insurance men or landlords. When they came, they arrive early on Saturday mornings with no regards to the fact that the men of the house had worked all week and deserved to sleep in late on Saturdays, especially, since the houses in our neighborhood were shot gun and provided no privacy for anyone. The white men didn't care. Such men would go to the white neighborhood at a decent time, but this particular white man used to walk through our neighborhood every Saturday morning with a sack on his back. He appeared to us never to have shaved. We used to run inside our respective houses until he was gone. I recalled how my heart would be pounding. After he was gone we would return outside where he would be our topic. I soon found out that my heart wasn't the only one that was pounding. We never pretended that we weren't afraid of someone when we knew we were. There was always honesty among us. The boys were more cowards than the girls. One day we came to a decision that this man was too much for us to keep to ourselves and decided that we should tell an adult about him. I think we put more fear upon ourselves about this man by talking about the "what ifs." I also believe that my mother had overheard our conversations and told the other parents. The adults waited for us to confront them with the issue at hand. We voted on whose parents we would talk to; of course everyone agreed that we would select my mother. We told her that we had a problem that we felt that the grown-ups should be aware of in case something happened to one of us. I never could understand how my mother could keep a straight face and sound so convincing. She allowed us to tell her about this white man that passed through the neighborhood every Saturday at nine o'clock in the morning. She asked me how I knew that the time was nine o'clock when he passed. I told her that I had looked at the clock for several weeks and it always showed nine o'clock. We told her that the man was mumbling something that we couldn't understand. My mother, someone that all of us loved and trusted so much told us that this man was saying: "Don't be scared to pass." She also told us that he had been coming through the neighborhood since she had been a little girl. I thought that fact was a bit too much considering that he looked only about ten years older then she. She added that she thought that he was in jail. She mumbled to herself but loud enough for us to hear ("They must have let him out"). She continued "to say that he goes around kidnapping children and putting them in his sack when they tried to pass him." His sack looked full when he had children inside of it. She told; Us that we were lucky to be smart enough to run and hide because he must have heard that our street had lots of children. My mother knew that she had our undivided attention and the more questions we asked her, the more she embellished her story. She knew that she had scared us half to death. Everything seemed to come together as to what she was saying. Someone asked her what the man did with all of the children. Her response was that he ate them. Her answer blew our mind, and she knew it. When our conversation with my mother was over we couldn't end there. That was the talk of the month or shall I say of the year.

I don't know whether our parents planned this incident to keep us from wandering from outside the neighborhood. If that was their plan, it worked. We stayed within the rims of our own neighborhood, with the exception of attending school across town. We traveled to school as a group and came home as a group. We were not allowed to leave anyone behind. As the years went by, our parents thought that our curiosity about that man was over. They couldn't have been further from the truth. We continued to clear the streets at nine o'clock in the morning until he passed. One Saturday when I was about thirteen or fourteen I suggested that we stay outside as a group until he passed. I believed that he couldn't kidnap all of us. Needlesstosay, everyone disagreed with me. I told them that I was tired of running from this man and that I wasn't running anymore. I told them that when he passed, I would stay there and everyone else could run home and look out of their windows. I suggested that if they saw him putting me in his bag to yell for our parents; I knew he wouldn't get too far. The time grew nearer for him to pass. I was both scared and curious. This man was coming down our street, and I could hear my teeth clicking together as he had moved closer to me. I decided to say "Good Morning" to him. He replied "Good Morning" young lady. I also had the opportunity to hear what he was mumbling. It wasn't "don't be scared to pass" as my mother had implied. He was saying "Sewing machine repair." Throughout all those years, our parents had known that this man was harmless, so they had allowed him to walk through our neighborhood. After this incident we realized that if our parents thought the man was a danger to us they would have called the authorities. As a group, we confronted my mother and all she could do was laugh. She said that she knew that we would learn the truth, but that was one to grow on. She added that she didn't think we would have taken so long to understand. We explained to her that we were scared half to death. After she apologized to us she reminded us that this kept us from wandering out of the neighborhood, a point which was quite true.

The Ball Snatcher

We were children that loved to play. Our favorite sport was baseball. Although, we appeared to have had an observer, the old man sitting on his porch and watching us play baseball was waiting for our ball to enter in his yard so that he could take it from us. Initially, we thought he was joking with us. Everyone called him Papa Joe. When we asked Papa Joe if we could have our ball back, his response was no. That was the beginning of years of lost baseballs. We told Mrs. White, who tried to get these balls from him; he told her that the balls were his. Papa Joe lived with his daughter and son-in-law. Suffering from Alzheimer, caused him to forget or sometimes regress. He would not give our balls back to us under any circumstances. The adults in our neighborhood knew how much we loved our baseball and taking it from us only when it went in his yard was Papa Joe's favorite pass time, so they kept us with an ample supply of baseballs. We tried not to let the ball go in Papa Joe's yard, but if by chance it did we decided that we would try to run in his yard and beat him to it. Therefore, we always had someone posted close to his yard. Sometimes we would beat him to the ball, but most of the time he would beat us. If we got to the ball first he would get so angry with us that he would curse all of us. This routine became part of his everyday activities, and I often thought that taking the ball from us helped him to live longer. He seemed to be getting self-gratification from taking our balls. He would not speak to us when we spoke to him, but his daughter told my mother that he would ask her whether "those chillins (children)" were going to play ball today. We then realized that Papa Joe did like us and that we were his entertainment. To see how intrigued he was with getting our ball, was gratifying. Sometimes I often wondered if we made an impact on Papa Joe's life. What would his life have been like had we not been dispatched there at that allotted time? The years went by and Papa Joe's Alzheimer and old age took its toll on him. One day, he was no longer able to run after our balls. Papa Joe was put in an ambulance and taken to the hospital. We found out later that he had suffered a stroke. He no longer appeared interested in our balls, because the stroke had left him paralyzed on his left side. Though, he still was our number one fan, we really missed his taking our balls. Papa Joe passed one month after his stroke, and our hearts were saddened. Mrs. Smith (Papa Joe's daughter), called us about five months after his death. She told us that she had something for us. She gave us a long footlocker which she told us to open. Inside the footlocker was filled with all of the balls that Papa Joe had taken from us over the years. We had not realized he had taken so many balls from us. Maybe, the number seemed small in comparison to what he had given us in return. We continued to play our softball in the street of our neighborhood, but the games did not seem the same without Papa Joe racing to get our ball. I suppose that there was a special but unspoken bond between Papa Joe and us.

Weird Happenings

Many people have heard of mysterious things that go on in the state of Louisiana. Believe them! My friends, my sister, brothers and I have encountered a few weird happenings in our times, ones we would never forget. Louisiana seems at times so dreary in the fall, starting around late September and early October. The weather starts to turn cool and it rains a lot during this time of the year. At this time weird things begin to happen, especially in the evening around dusk. I remembered one evening my mother had sent my brother to the store to get a loaf of bread. Our friend Sandra had gone with him. They came back from the store in a panic. These children were running so fast that my brother hit against the door of the house because he couldn't stop. The impact caused my mother to immediately rush to the door to see the reason for all of the commotion. When she opened the door my brother and Sandra ran into her arms scared to death. I had never seen two black people's complextion change to another color. These children were frightened to death; something or someone had surely frightened them. My mother tried to calm them down to hear what they were trying to tell her, but they weren't making any sense. Their eyes were bulging out of their heads. My mother finally calmed them down, but they continued to talk at the same time. All we could hear them say at the same time was that they had seen a man. When my mother asked them why the man had disturbed them or was he trying to hurt them, simultaneously, they said "no." My mother asked if something was wrong with the man. In unison they yelled that "the man had no head." Apparently, they had been coming from the store, talking to each other, when they noticed a man, dressed in dark clothing with no head, standing on the other side of the street. Such an incident was not uncommon in our community during the wintertime. That night, it was raining. The adults didn't take such things lightly; the men took my brother and our friend back to the store to investigate. Of course the man wasn't there. I'm glad that our parents took seriously the things we said. They never told us to sit down because of our imagination. Perhaps because we never gave them reason to doubt us.

This incident started the adults talking about other strange happenings. They remembered how one of my mother's cousin had been coming from work one evening when she saw a cat on that same street. They remembered that Cousin Mary stated that she was wondering where that little kitten came from because no one in our neighborhood had a kitten or couldn't afford to have one. She said that the closer she got to our block, the bigger the kitten became until he was a full grown cat. Then it disappeared before her eyes. She frantically ran to my mother's house. My father and others had tried to calm her down, but she wasn't making any sense. When they understood that she was saying something about a cat, my mother told her that there weren't any cats in our neighborhood. She told them that she knew that there weren't any cats in our neighborhood. However, she insisted that she had seen a cat and that it had gone from being a kitten to a full-grown cat before disappearing before her eyes.

In another incident we were playing in the yard when we heard a car crash. We went inside to inform my mother of the car crash. We asked her if we could go to the place of the accident. Not only did she refuse our request, but what was so bad about it was that all of us heard her, also our curiosity got the best of us. My mother was busy taking care of my older brother's headache. While she had him to lie on the sofa as she got a pillow, a cold towel and some aspirins for his head, we decided that we would have time to investigate the accident and return before my mother even realized we were gone. We learned a valuable lesson on that day. The lesson was that obedience is good.

As we made our way to the scene of the accident, we looked directly into the face of the same brother who had been on the sofa with the headache. He stopped us before we could see the accident to remind and ask us that our mother had told us all not to come here. He warned us that we had better beat him home. Believe me we did just that. There were several things that were really strange about my brother's being there. My brothers, sister, friends and I sat on our back porch and discussed it. The first thing we all agreed on was that my brother could not have driven to the accident and beaten us there, because we had taken a short cut through the back fence. He couldn't have driven his car because the traffic was backed up. Secondly, we had seen my brother lying on the sofa in excruciating pain, moaning and groaning. Then he had been in no condition to spank any kids. Yet, this person who appeared to be my brother was talking about what he was going to do to us if he got home before we did. Thirdly, his clothes were a different color from those worn by the brother who had been lying on the sofa. I had always admired the way my brother dressed. He has always worn hats that matched his pants and socks to match his shirts. Since, blue is my favorite color that color stuck in mind. My brother had worn dark blue pants and hat, a light blue shirt and matching socks. The person that we had thought was my brother wore dark brown pants and hat, a beige shirt and socks. Every one of us had seen what the man at the scene of the accident had on, so we could easily prove what my brother had worn. We had gone inside to investigate my brother's attire as he slept. As I looked back, I guess that six kids peeking at a sleeping man did look strange. My mother asked what were we doing and told us not to make any noise because my brother was asleep. We told her that we wanted to see the color of his clothes. He indeed wore blue. We asked my mother if Timothy left the house, but she informed us that he hadn't. Having a mother so in tune to us, we knew that questioning and strange behavior made her curious. She said we were acting as if we had seen a ghost. She didn't realize that her statement was the understatement of the year, until we told her what had happened. She said that what we had seen was my brother's spirit warning us. We wondered how a person's spirit could roam around when the person is alive. She explained that she didn't know if such an act was a phenomenon, or an unexplainable incident or situation. We didn't get into trouble for having been disobedient because mom said we had been punished enough with fright. Can you imagine how eerie that experience was; especially for children? Consequently, the man or spirit had done us a favor by running us home. The accident had been indeed a gruesome one. Three men traveling in a sports car that lost control and went under a large truck killing all of the occupants. We knew the victims. Even more disturbing was that my brother- in- law had been riding with those men. He had been dropped off at home to take a shower with the intent for them to pick him up later. The authorities stated that if my brother- in –law had been in the car, the impact would have cut his neck off due to his height. Someone reported, "One of the victims was scalped, cutting off the top of his head." Sometimes being curious doesn't pay because curiosity can be haunting. But what is a girl to do if her inquiring mind wants to know.

School Days

Unlike the school system today, when I was growing up, the teachers' were in control of their classrooms. Discipline in the classrooms was enforced. The teachers were allowed to spank the students during this era. Morning prayers were recited before class started along with the pledge of allegiance, all of which, contrary to popular belief, made a difference in the actions of the students. In an article on the Top Seven Disciplinary Problems in U. S. Schools, the source was (Congressional Quarterly Researcher), the article compares the disciplinary problems of the U.S. Schools from the 1940s' to the schools in the 1990s:

1940's	1990's
1. Talking Out of Turn	1. Drug Abuse
2. Chewing Gum	2. Alcohol Abuse
3. Making Noise	3. Pregnancy
4. Running in the Halls	4. Suicide
5. Cutting in line	5. Rape
6. Dress Code Violations	6. Robbery
7. Littering	7. Assault

I thought about how blessed the administration and teachers were to have such disciplinary problems as those identified in the 1940's, though some were considered major violations. Who would have imagined that today's children would abuse drugs and alcohol;

Or that teen pregnancy, students' killing, bomb threats, assaulting teachers would have crept into the U.S. School system as revealed in the mid-90's and 2000's.

Among the disciplinary problems, which were more or less the same during my era of the 1950's were the problem with integration of schools in the late sixties. I recalled when the schools were segregated. Black students from across town were bused to the school in our neighborhood. The classrooms were over crowded but discipline was still enforced. I also recall that one little girl, Mary Black was among those transported. She was a very hateful little girl that was very short. I must have stood at least a foot taller than she. This little girl didn't like me at all, but I was scared to death of this little midget. In class, she sat behind me. I had very long hair and hers was very short. She used to pull my hair, put her feet in my chair, kicked me on my bottom, take my lunch and milk money. I would rather have gone up against the whole school to fight than to fight this little girl. I didn't know why I was so afraid of her. I didn't tell anyone about what she was doing to me. If I had told the teacher, she would have quickly stopped the girl's actions. I was so glad when those children returned to their own school. Someone had set their school on fire, and some repairs had to be completed before the students could return. The principal didn't want the students to miss so many days from school, so he arranged with our principal for them to be taught at to our school. Their teachers arrived at our school also, but our teachers were the primary teachers since their classrooms were used. Teachers were serious about teaching and educating the students was their number one priority. The teachers carried the big stick, which they didn't mind using. If students got out of hand they would use the big stick called "The Pointer." Then, they were allowed to spank the students. For instance if the students were talking in class after they had been forewarned, the teacher would have them to hold out their hands and receive a swat on the palm with the pointer. The pointer didn't feel good at all. Though we became angry with our teacher, we knew not to let the anger show. If the discipline problem was as serious as students hitting each other, the result required cloakroom action. Therefore, the teacher would take these students to the cloakroom to give them one swat on their bottoms. We never felt embarrassed because we never laughed at each other. The teachers controlled the school and their classroom with the principal getting involved as the last resort. No one wanted to go to the principal's office. I always pictured going to the principal's office as going to jail, and I didn't want to experience either.

Integration of Schools

Then came the integration of schools. I would never forget it because we were among the first set of black students to be integrated and the experience wasn't nice. The teachers didn't make our journey into this different dimension any easier. Walking into someone's house and not feeling welcome is hard, but the options are staying and being miserable or simply leaving. Being ordered to go to a school at a place that's not a preference and not being welcome is different. I noticed that the white students weren't forced to go to the schools in the black neighborhood. The first year of integration was very chaotic; we were trying to adjust; hatred toward us escalated among the white teachers and students alike. The students hurled racial slurs at us constantly sometimes in front of the teachers but they received no punishments. These actions breathed resentment among the students and tension built up; fights broke out among the students. The black students were suspended and the white students parents were called. Nevertheless, the white students were allowed to stay in school. I asked my mother repeatly to get me out of that school, but she encouraged me to remain. The black adults didn't like confrontations with their white counterparts. I don't think they tried to avoid confrontations with their white counterparts out of fear, but perhaps, because of the injustices and inequalities that would result for them. One time my mother and I attended a conference with the counselor and principal of my school because I had questioned my teacher about the black students' being suspended and not the other students. The teacher refused to answer the question; however, she did send me to the counselor who in turn took me to the principal.

He asked me why was I creating trouble in the classroom. He was the most racist and unjust person I had ever encountered; but I told him that I had only asked her a simple question. My mother experienced first hand the situation that I complained about. The principal insisted that my mother had too many children, and that fact explained the reason I acted as I did. He also suggested that she might want to think about taking me to see a psychiatrist. Then my mother allowed him to finish analyzing me; she let him have it. She told him that she had eleven children instead of the three that were attending his school, and that he was the first person to criticize her on the upbringing of her children. She pointed out that he had just met her and that he didn't know anything about her. He tried to apologize, but he had angered my mother in a way that I had never seen and didn't ever want to see again. This principal's face turned so red that I felt sorry for the poor man. My mother also informed him that the teachers had driven me to the point that I wanted to go to another school. She told him that segregated schools were no longer legal so he needed adjust. I had thought the woman was afraid to speak out to white people, but I realized that she was afraid that she might be pushed too far, if she ever had a confrontation with them. I had never seen my mother become upset because she's usually the peacemaker. I tried to thank her for defending me. I told her how proud I was that she had defended me to that principal. I thought about how silly I had been to try to hold a conversation with this woman when I saw what appeared to me to be steam coming from her ears. When I realized what I had done, I tried to swallow my words but I was too late. My mother turned and looked at me with the most disgusted look. She told me that if it had not been for me, she wouldn't have been at that school in the first place. She said nothing more to me; she walked away and left me standing there in a state of shock. I came home from school that evening and she still wasn't talking to me. I guess she did have a right to be angry with me. I apologized to her and promised her that I would try to control my temper. She accepted my apology and gave me a hug. Despite my promise, the teachers remained racists. I thought school would never end. Needless to say I was retained with an eighty- two average because, as the teacher told my mother the reason for retaining me was because of my behavior.

The Transfer

My mother used my aunt's address as a means to transfer us to an all black school. When the counselor saw my grades he called me to his office. He told me to tell my parents to take my report card to the school board because I should not be retained because of my behavior. After my mother heard what the counselor said, I became excited with that good news. I reminded my mother everyday to go to the school board, and everyday she would tell me that she was going to go the next day. That day never came, so

I had to repeat the seventh grade. My anger with my mother lasted years before I forgave her. While in the seventh grade, I had an English teacher that I thought was the meanest person in the world. Though, she was a good teacher, I think her purpose in life was to make the students' lives miserable. Her classroom was the quietest in the entire school. She would say that she didn't want to hear a pin drop. If I had had a straight pin, I would have dropped it, just to see her response. One would think that the classroom was empty until the door opened only to find Miss Drew and about thirty students. She spoke very softly into a microphone because she said that she didn't want to strain her voice. Everyone had to be sitting in his or her respective seats before the second bell rang. If we weren't in her class before that second bell, she said; "Don't bother to come especially without a pass from the office." As faith would have it another student and I arrived inside the room just as the second bell rang because we had stopped to get some water. The other student told Ms. Drew that we had been thirsty. I also informed her that we were inside the class when the second bell rang. We couldn't afford to miss this class because we were reviewing for the upcoming test. She told us to get a pass. I asked her how could we, get a pass since we had been at water fountain. She told me to find the answer to my question and that we had better not come back without a pass. Therefore, Joanne and I went back to the water fountain where I took out a sheet of paper. When Joanne ask me what was I doing, I informed her that I was writing a note to get us back in class. The note read: "Please excuse Toni and Joanne for being late to class. They needed to visit me. Sign: Mr. Water Fountain." The situation wouldn't have been so bad if she hadn't read the note aloud. The class started laughing so uncontrollably that she couldn't get the order back in class. This day was the first time anyone had ever heard noise coming out of her class and the last time. Teachers from other classes came to investigate. Miss Drew was so upset with us she started to cry. After she asked one of the other teachers to watch her class, she took us to the office. We were suspended for three days. I felt so bad because I had made the old witch cry, but I wanted to get the test review. I started to get nervous because I knew I had to face my mother. She gave me a spanking and put me on punishment for what seemed like eternity. On top of the ordeal, I had to apologize to Miss Drew, an act which I didn't mind performing. Joanne didn't get on punishments or spankings.

When I returned to class I was among the first few that were sitting down in Miss Drew's class. Believe me, she didn't have any more trouble out of me. If I became thirsty I went to class and then after we were settled I raised my hand and asked her for permission to get some water. I must admit that when I was growing up I sometimes took leave of my senses and did stupid things, such as the water fountain incident. The irony is that I wasn't doing those things to be funny, but thank God my mother knew how to bring me back to my senses. She knew how to keep all of us in line; my father, on the other hand, was very lenient.

In the same school year, I can recall that, one of our teachers had gone on strike for a raise. She was the only teacher in the whole district that was on strike. She walked around our school all day for about two weeks with her picket sign. No one bothered her, and she spoke not a word to any one. The students admired what she was doing and decided to picket with her on that Friday. Mrs. May had no idea what our intentions were. We made our own picket signs, joined in with Mrs. May, and walked around the school. Needlesstosay no students went to class that day. By Monday the strike was over and Mrs. May and the rest of the teachers received their over due and much-deserved raise.

Rain, Rain, Don't Go Away

As I stated earlier, the children in our little community should have been in the world book of geniuses for being the most naive children in that era. Many of the things that we decided to do didn't make any sense. Moreover, we always discussed what ever we were going to do as a group. The majority of the time we all agreed. Ironically, some of our foolish acts were really farfetched and not one of us noticed just how farfetched they were. Picture this: during the fall season of the year. Our city got most of its rain. It rained like cats and dogs the whole weekend. In fact, early that Monday morning, the rain was still pouring down with lightning and thundering continuing until about 5:30 a.m. Now, all of the children knew that this kind of rain meant <u>NO SCHOOL</u>. Unfortunately, we were very disappointed that the rain stopped before 7 o'clock. As a result, we had to go to school. To get there, we rode the public buses. We walked three long blocks to get to the bus stop, so in all of our minds, we knew that we couldn't have arrived at school even if school had been opened. Needlesstosay, we were angry children walking slowly to the bus stop. The topic for that morning was how angry we were at the rain for stopping before it was time for us to go to school. We had to ride two buses and walk a block to get to our school, but, as fate would have it one building with a broken gutter had water still pouring down. The rain looked as though it was still falling. Keep in mind that there were nine of us from my neighborhood and remember that we didn't do anything without discussing, and agreeing that either all of us would do it or one of us would and everyone else would support that person. We knew that all nine of us had to return home together or none of us could go home. Since all of us had the mindset of staying home, in the first place we agreed to stand under that gutter and get soaked. We did so but unfortunately we caught the bus with the same driver that had dropped us off. He wanted to know what had happened to us but we ignored his question. He didn't insist because he knew what we had done. We arrived at our destination. Some of the parents were outside and saw us coming down the street. Someone yelled! "What are you all doing back home?" One of us yelled that we had gotten wet on our way to school. We walk toward them soaking wet. One of the parents asked how were you all so wet when the sun is beaming down. All of us just stood there looking stupid. Finally someone said that the rain was falling by the school. Well, one of the parents told us to change our clothes while she called the school to let someone know that we would be late because we had to come change our wet clothes. The adults sent us back to school and dealt with us when we came home. All of us were on punishment for a month.

In another silly incident I talked my sister into doing. Remember that we didn't do anything without the consent of everyone involved. If one person didn't agree, we didn't do it. Well, my sister and I were on punishment for another reason. In this rare instance, mom left us at home without adult supervision, so that she could go to the grocery store. My overactive mind started to work, and I suggested to my sister that we should call a cab to every house in our neighborhood. She thought that was a good idea, so we took turns calling. But we obviously had forgotten that we were part of the neighborhood and didn't call a cab to our house. My brother who was a year older than I came in the house to ask us why we called all of those cabs. We denied any knowledge about the cabs. He had always called me a weasel face when he became angry with me, but that name did not bother me until I looked in the dictionary to see what a weasel looked like. Then I developed a complex, which I later overcame. Nonetheless, he said that he had understood our plan when he noticed that a cab came to every house except ours. He thought that his duty was to tell our mom since he was the oldest. Trying to bribe him with his favorite candy did not work. Consequently, we were spanked, had to admit that we had called the cabs in the neighborhood, and had to apologize to each of them. The whole incident was very humiliating, in addition to our punishment. All of this unpleasantness could have been avoided if the boy had taken the candy and kept his mouth closed.

Pranks Can Back Fire

There were another incident months later, one that would haunt me for the rest of my life. Even today, when I think about it tears form in my eyes, or when I hear someone say that a person has to leave because his or her mother is sick, something swells inside of me. One of our neighborhood children and I had after school detention because she was clowning in class, and I laughed at her. We arrived at detention on time. We were supposed to be there no more than fifteen minutes, but Sandra came there making funny noises. I refused to get into any more trouble. The teacher allowed me to leave five minutes earlier because I was quiet. I think that I was sitting quietly because I was worried that I had to face my mother. I knew she had gotten the word about my detention by now. Sometimes we do not think about the consequences until after the fact. I stood outside the door waiting for Sandra when our teacher noticed me and told me to go home. I said that Sandra and I had to walk home together. She told me Sandra still had five more minutes. Obviously, Sandra thought that five minutes was too long. She came up with an idea for me to tell the teacher that her mother had come to pick us up. Mrs. White knew that Sandra was telling me what to say, so her response to me was to tell Sandra's mother that she had to wait or leave. Then Sandra came up with another brilliant idea, so we thought. She told me to tell the teacher that an emergency had taken place. Sandra's father is in the hospital. I repeated what Sandra had told me to say and the teacher let her go. I don't know if Mrs. White released Sandra because her time was up or because of the lie we had told her. Nevertheless, we walked home and Sandra was pleased with what we had done. On the other hand, I was feeling so bad that we had resorted to lying to the teacher. What we had done bothered me so much, that I was in this **"WHAT IF"** state. I recalled asking her; "what if" we had left earlier than we were supposed to leave and there had been an accident, or **"what if"** a car had hit one of us? What was the other person to do or how could we explain this incident to the other one's family? How could the other one live with herself, knowing the truth? "What if" the lie that we told the teacher turned out to be true and her father was really in the hospital; how would we live with ourselves? She told me that her father was all right because he was at work. I had a weird feeling all the way home. I couldn't explain how I was feeling, but I told Sandra that we needed to hurry home. She asked me why I was acting so weird and looked so serious. I couldn't explain, nor could I explain the funny feeling that I had inside of me. I supposed I felt a sickening feeling, but I didn't know why.

We had found a bowling ball on our way home and Sandra wanted to kick it home, about two and a half miles from school. She thought that maybe kicking the bowling ball would help relax me, so we kicked that ball all the way home. I was thinking to myself that this day had been the weirdest I've ever seen. We finally arrived home; we arrived at Sandra's house first. When she entered her house, I kept on walking to my house. I could hear her screaming; I thought that her mother must have met her at the door and spanked her for having detention. I immediately dismissed that thought because her cry didn't sound like it had come from a spanking. Sandra screamed and kept on saying "Oh! No!"

When I walked into my house it was quiet and appeared that everyone had been crying. I asked why everyone was looking so sad as if someone had died. When my mother said someone had died - Mr. Bruce, I thought I would die. My mother had a hard time with me. I think I must have taken his death just as hard as his children did. When I told my mother that I had to go to Sandra, she didn't understand and I didn't wait for her approval. Apparently, Sandra was thinking the same thing that she needed to get to me because we met in the middle of the street and cried so hard. I couldn't stop apologizing to her. I told her that if only I hadn't listened to her and told the teacher that her father was in the hospital, this tragedy wouldn't have happened to Mr. Bruce. She tried to assure me that his death wasn't my fault. She informed me that her mother said Mr. Bruce had been in the hospital since earlier that morning. He had gone to work but had passed out at work. He had gone into a coma after a blood vessel had popped in his head. He had never regained consciousness. Mr. Bruce had died at the exact time that I was telling the teacher that he was in the hospital. I made a vow never to pretend that anyone's parents were sick in order to have my way. I promised to accept any consequences that came my way. The adults in the neighborhood told Sandra and me that Mr. Bruce's time had come because God had called him home. They assured us that he would have died on that particular day at that precise time even if we hadn't told the teacher that he was in the emergency room. My friend had to grow up fast. She had to help take care of her little sister and brother while her mother worked. She had older sisters, but they had their own lives. Her mother seemed to have drifted into her own world after her husband died. Sandra eventually quit school in her junior year in order to get a job and take care of her little brother and sister. Two years after the death of her father, her mother walked away from the family never to be seen or heard from again. She left all of her clothes behind which made them think that foul play occurred. The family took all of the appropriate measures in filing a missing person report. The missing person report was to no avail; their mother seemed to have vanished from the face of the earth without a trace. Sandra met an older man and they married. He encouraged her to get her diploma; she was given the opportunity to graduate from high school and she took it. My dear friend eventually became a successful businesswoman. Today, she is still married to Larry. She said that she would forever be indebted to Larry for giving her life back to her. Larry didn't want her to feel indebted to him. He just wanted her love. They had two children. I was so glad that something good had come out of our stupidity. Thirty something years have passed since we lied to that teacher, but through all of the trials and tribulations that life has taken me through, that incident is one I will never forget. It has the same impact on me today as it did that day we found out that her father had died. When I hear young people joking about their parents in the same manner as Sandra and I did, I take that opportunity to tell them about this incident.

The School Janitor

Times have changed. I can recall when our elementary school had only one janitor. This man was well respected by everyone. When he cleaned the restroom, the students and teachers alike made a minimum amount of mess. If one spilled water on the floor one would have had to wipe it up. We knew that we had only one janitor and the principal clearly established that the janitor wouldn't be over worked. The principal expected that we would treat our school as we treated our homes because it was our home away from home. I think cleanliness was contagious at our school because even the students that didn't live in very clean homes pitched in and kept the school clean. I also recalled that our school ground had a house that was fenced in on the school premises. Our janitor and his family lived there free of charge with all utilities paid by the school. The stipulation was that he had to take care of the entire school (the grounds, fix any type of wear and tear, painting, sweeping, mopping and waxing etc.). Mr. Willie, our janitor was well liked by everyone. He lived with his wife and three children. Our two-story building school had lots of classrooms, and Mr. Willie was responsible for cleaning every room. He was on call during school hours in case there was a spillage too big for the students or teachers to handle. I have never seen the principal or any of the teachers' look down on Mr. Willie as though he was beneath them. Our school appearance was beautiful inside and out, thanks to our janitor. Our landscape was always well groomed. What I liked is that Mr. Willie's whole family pitched in to help him around the school. Amazingly the janitor as was true for everyone else back then were not getting paid much, yet, they had given one hundred percent effort on their jobs and their effort showed. But today the school janitors, called custodians, and work as a team of five or six instead of one person. I take my hat off and salute Mr. Willie and all of the janitors of old who kept our schools cleaned and as germ free as possible, and to the custodians who are doing like wise today, I thank all of you.

The Janitor's Wife

I remembered that Mr. Willie's wife sold the best, frozen cups or icebergs as we used to call them, when the weather started to get warm. The frozen cups were made from fruity flavor syrup of all flavors. She sold root beer, pineapple, strawberry, and cherry. You named it, she had it. If by chance she didn't have what we wanted, all we had to do was tell her and she would have it the next day. The school allowed us to buy frozen cups during our lunch break and after school; the teachers bought theirs at time. If a teacher wanted to buy one during class time, he or she would have to buy one for the whole class; otherwise, the teacher was not allowed to eat in front of the students. Many teachers have honored that request and have actually bought frozen cups for the whole class. I realized that we were actually Mrs. Ruby's advertisement, because our parents wanted to know why we wanted to have frozen cups everyday. Needless to say the adults were hooked, too. Even though we knew Mrs. Lucy's name we use to call her Miss Frozen cup lady, a name that never made her anger. She would greet us with a smile. Mrs. Lucy sold her frozen cups seven days a week. She sold them during lunchtime and after school during the school year, as early as ten o'clock on weekdays and Saturdays; and after church on Sundays (about 1 o'clock). Our parents would sometimes walk with us to get the frozen cups in the summer, when the weather was breezy. Buying the frozen cups was so much fun, when the adults were in our presence, though they would be laughing and talking among themselves.

As I look back to the yesteryears, I realize that everything the people in our community and surroundings had done came from their heart. Mrs. Lucy put so much love and devotion into her frozen cups, yet she charged only a nickel for them. Today many, people just throw anything together and would charge an arm and a leg for it. Sometimes one person would buy ten or fifteen frozen cups at a times. Our parents would give us bags for the frozen cups. We would round up everyone's money to make one trip for the whole neighborhood. We walked about eight blocks to Mrs. Lucy's house, but the trip was well worth our time. Buying the cups were our treats in the evening after we had taken our bath and put on clean clothes during the summertime. Mrs. Lucy and their children even pitched in and help Mr. Willie clean the school. In those days, there were mutual respect among the family members. Somehow, in our society some changes occurred and the janitors' houses on the school campus disappeared. The janitor was replaced with a staff of janitors and the quality of services diminished. My motto is "if it isn't broken, don't try to fix it".

The Breaking Up of Our Community
....

The children in our community had started to out grow the spaces in the houses. Because of our growth our parents had to look for houses with more rooms. This change meant the breaking up of our community. Some of us kept in contact. However, the Bazils seemed to have vanished from the face of the earth; no one knew where they had moved. As we had gotten older the Bazils had started to resurface. Obviously, the abuse the children in this family endured surely had a negative effect on most them as adults. The two sons stayed in and out of jail for car theft. The oldest son was obsessed with cars and made a hobby of stealing cars, fixing them up and driving them. David eventually taught his younger brother, Larry how to steal cars. They had finally gotten the picture that going around stealing other people's car was illegal. They were reformed after being in and out of jail. They went to the job corps, taken up a trade in auto mechanics, graduated and "came home" to get jobs as mechanics. Eventually, they opened up their own mechanic shop. David had gotten married but was very abusive to his wife and children. The two oldest daughters (Janice and Kate) had nervous breakdowns before the age of thirty, resulting in the state getting custody of their children. Janice had thyroid disease that caused her eyes to bulge out. She died in the bar room after drinking while taking the medication for her thyroid and nerves. The two middle daughters ran away from home. The youngest, of the two middle daughters ended up in California, met and married an older man with six children: though, they weren't her biological children but she adopted them. After a few years of being married to this abusive man she divorced him and was awarded custody of the children. Marion is an example of someone who was abused as a child, not becoming an abuser. She sought counseling for the children and herself. She left California, with the children and returned home. She never went back to her parents' home. Marion received her degree in Social Work and began to work with Child Protective Services. She vowed that no other child would be abused if she could help it. The other middle sister Tynia was never heard from again. The two youngest Terry and Brenda were as scarred as the two older sisters were. Terri's boyfriend (Bobby), shot and killed Brenda, and shot Terri in the abdomen and left hip and leg. When the two sisters confronted him about stealing their mother's rent money from her. According to Brenda's mother, he had shot Brenda three times, twice in the chest and once in the head. Mrs. Bazil lived next door to Terri and was going to investigate the disturbance, when she saw her daughter running out of the house down the street. Mrs. Bazil stated that she was in hot pursuit calling Brenda's name, trying to get her to stay still. She finally collapsed within a half block from her mother's house. Brenda died in her mother's arm after asking her mother to take care of her son. Terri's boyfriend left, but he was apprehended at his sister's house, where he was looking at television and drinking a beer. His sister knew nothing about the crime he had committed two hours ago. Bobby's mother called the police after he had confessed what he had done to her. Mrs. Myner told Bobby he couldn't stay there. After, about two hours she had decided to turn her son over to the police. Though this decision was the hardest thing to do, it was the right thing to do. Mrs. Myner had thought Bobby would visit his sister's house. She decided to call her daughter to see if her son was there. Of course he was there just as his mother suspected. Mrs. Myner told Cynithia what had transpired, and asked her to keep the call anonymous from him. She told Cynthia not to confront him about the situation because he was dangerous and could hurt her. She asked her daugther to try to keep him there. She sent the police to Cynthia's house where Bobby was still looking at television. At first, he denied shooting Terri and Brenda; then he confessed to the shootings. The police placed him under arrest and took him down to the station. Then they went to the hospital to talk Terri, who refused to talk to them or testify against her boyfriend. One of the bullets had damaged her intestine. She has to wear a bag for the rest of her life, the ligaments in her left leg were damaged causing her to throw her hip when she walks. One could only imagine the turmoil that was wailing inside of her. This young woman was lying in the hospital, fighting for her life, realizing that the man she loved put her there and that he had shot her sister. Terri wasn't told that Brenda had died at the time she refused to talk to the police. The doctors thought that she was too weak to handle the news. She kept asking about her sister because she knew Brenda was shot also. She didn't know how bad the situation had been. Terri had been shot first when Brenda tried to take the gun from Bobby. Therefore, he turned it on Terri. He shot her at close range with a 38 caliber. The doctors could not understand how she had run as far as she did. They thought that she should have died instantly, given the way the bullet pierced her heart and the way she had been shot in the head at close range. A terrible tragedy had occurred for the family and the neighbors in our old neighborhood.

There is a saying that people can sometimes sense their own death, and such seemed to be the case with Brenda. The day before she was killed, she had gone into the old neighborhood to see all of the old neighbors. She seemed to have been on a pilgrimage, and she spent that whole day visiting the neighbor. When she finally arrived at my mother's house, my mother said we had just missed each other. According to my mother, Brenda had become very upset that she missed seeing me. The strange way Brenda was acting disturbed my mother to the point that she called me at work. She said that Brenda came by and said needed to talk to me, regardless of the time. This request was strange because I hadn't talk to Brenda in about two years. After work I went to my mother's house to pick up my daughter; of course my mother reminded me to call Brenda, but, the time was late 10:30 P. M.. I was eight month's pregnant, but I promised I would call Brenda later that day. I remembered telling my mother that Brenda wasn't going anywhere; she would be right there when I wake up. When I arrived at my mother's house a little after noon, my mother met me at the door. The look on her face told me that something was wrong. I knew my suspicion was right when she told me to sit down. Immediately I asked her what was wrong. She told me Mrs. Gray had received a frantic called from Marion, in between sobs, Mrs. Gray heard that someone had been shot Mrs. Gray asked her to try to calm down so she could understand what she was saying. She told Marion, that she heard her said that someone was shot, but she couldn't make out whom. Marion tried to calm herself down and told her that Terri's boyfriend had shot Terri and Brenda, and that Brenda was dead. I started crying uncontrollably, thinking how quickly one could lose his or her life. The words I had spoken to my mother hours ago in reference to Brenda being there when I wake up, echoed in my head. I immediately started wondering, what she could have needed to talk to me about. I wondered could she have been interested in spending time with me and joking around as we had done in the pass, or could she have simply needed some encouraging words that I had given to her in the past. What ever she had wanted, I finally realized that I would never ever know. I also realized that I needed to stop torturing myself. Brenda knew that she could have asked me for anything and I would have done it for her. No one knows the day or the hour he or she would depart from this earth. I thank God, for comforting me and relieving the guilt that I carried around with the "if only I"... I realized now that her death had been determined by God's plan. Even if I had returned her phone call, her demise had been predestined.

About the Author

My name is Thop Brown. I am a native of the state of Louisiana now living in Harker Heights, Texas. I am one of eleven children. I am the Wife of P. G. Brown Jr. and Mother of Tyn, Chelle (Baby girl) and Ty Brown. I am a Christian, a Gulf War Veteran (served in the United States Army), a graduate of the University of Central Texas with a Bachelor of Social Work degree, I'm formerly a Special Education Teacher worked with severely and profoundly disabled students. When I'm not writing I enjoy reading books, playing a good game of Volleyball, Coaching Volleyball at the Boys & Girls Club or dominoes, occasionally going to the movies and eating out. I have a very simple life and I love it.

Printed in Great Britain
by Amazon